Ten Items or Less

A Counting Book

By Stephanie Calmenson
Illustrated by Terri Super

A GOLDEN BOOK • NEW YORK
Western Publishing Company, Inc., Racine, Wisconsin 53404

Mandy liked shopping with her mommy. She liked to sit in the supermarket wagon and ride up and down the aisles.

When her mommy couldn't find things,
Mandy helped her.

"Do you see the cookies we like?" Mommy
asked.

Mandy looked on the shelves for the orange
box with a picture of a clown juggling cookies.
She saw red boxes, yellow boxes, green boxes ....
"There they are!" she called, pointing all the
way to the top shelf.

"Thank you," said Mommy. She put an orange box in the wagon. Then she asked, "Would you like to play a counting game today?"

"Oh, yes!" said Mandy. "I'm good at counting."
"Then you'll be good at this game," said
Mommy. "It's called 'Ten Items or Less.'"
Mandy looked puzzled. "What are 'items'?"
she asked.

"That's just another word for things," Mommy explained. "If you have ten items or less in your wagon, you get to check out on the express line." Then she added, "'Express' is another word for fast."

"We already have a box of cookies," Mandy said. "That's one thing!"

"And what would you like for dinner?" asked Mommy.

"Spaghetti!" answered Mandy. So they took a box of spaghetti from the shelf.

"That's two things," Mandy counted.

At the fruit section, Mr. Robbins was unpacking a big crate of watermelon.

"Let's have watermelon for dessert. Daddy loves watermelon," said Mommy. She put a piece in the wagon. That made three things.

Down the next aisle, Mandy saw the cereal she had eaten for breakfast at Grandma's house. It was called Munchy Crunchy Morning.

"Can we get that cereal?" Mandy asked. Mommy read the box to see what was inside. "It looks good," she said. So they put a box of Munchy Crunchy Morning in their wagon. That was four things.

"I like raisins in it, too," said Mandy.

"We have no raisins at home," Mommy said. "I'm glad you reminded me."

"That's five things!" called Mandy when her mommy put a box of raisins in the wagon.

Milk made six.

Cheese made seven.

Then Mandy remembered something important. It was her job to feed Max, the cat. And she remembered that his food was almost gone. "We need a bag of cat food," she said. That made eight things.

"I don't think we need much more," said
Mommy. "Let's look around to see if we forgot
anything."

In a corner of the store, they found mops and sponges and brooms.

"Daddy says we need a new broom," said Mommy. "You can pick one, Mandy."

Mandy picked out a broom with a yellow handle. It was fun to have a broom in the wagon. Mandy had to hold it tight so the broom wouldn't sweep everything off the shelves. "That's nine things," she said. "Are we ready to go?"

"We're ready!" answered Mommy.

They went right to the express line. Only three people were ahead of them. On the other lines, it looked like there were a hundred.

    While they waited their turn, Mandy looked
at the books.
    "You've been such a good helper," said
Mommy, "and we can still buy one more thing.
Is there a book you'd like?"
    "I'd like that one!" said Mandy, pointing to a
book with a saggy baggy elephant on the cover.
"And that makes ten things!" she added proudly.

Mandy and her mommy were next. "Do you
have ten items or less?" asked Mrs. Green at
the cash register.

"Yes, we do, Mrs. Green," said Mommy.
"Why don't you count for us, Mandy?"

Mandy counted while Mrs. Green added up the prices.

"One...two...three...four...five...six... seven...eight...nine...ten! We have ten items!" Mandy said.

"You're good at counting," Mrs. Green said as she put their things into a big brown bag. She handed the bag to Mommy. "See you again soon!" she said.

"Yes," Mandy said. "We'll see you every time we play 'Ten Items or Less.'"